London in a
Weekend with
Two Kids

*A Step-By-Step Travel Guide
About What to See and Where to
Eat
(Amazing Family-Friendly Things
to Do in London When You Have
Little Time)*

By

Hassan Osman

London in a Weekend with Two Kids: A Step-By-Step Travel Guide About What to See and Where to Eat (Amazing Family-Friendly Things to Do in London When You Have Little Time)
Copyright © 2019 by Hassan Osman.

Liability Disclaimer and FTC Notice
The purpose of this book is to provide the user with general information about the subject matter presented. This book is for entertainment purposes only. This book is not intended, nor should the user consider it, to be legal advice for a specific situation. The author, company, and publisher make no representations or warranties with respect to the accuracy, fitness, completeness, or applicability of the

Table of Contents

Introduction

London can be quite overwhelming with kids.

There is so much to do and see that you can go overboard on the planning.

Last summer, I spent a few days in London with my wife and two little girls (aged ten and six), and we had a fantastic time. We visited everything we wanted to visit in a short period.

This book is a short guide that will help you plan your trip. You get a step-by-step weekend itinerary with pointers about what to do and where to eat. You'll also get food recommendations and must-see highlights to make it a great trip for you and your kids.

Quick side note: If you've read any of my other books, "Rome in a Weekend with Two Kids" or "Paris in a Weekend with Two Kids," you'll find a lot of the early material in this book quite similar. That's because a lot of the planning methods, phone applications, and things to buy are mostly similar across

Europe. You can skip ahead to the itinerary if you'd like to save some time.

Why Read This Book?

I'm not an expert on travel, and I'm definitely not an expert on London.

So why read a book written by a novice like me?

Here are three reasons why:

1) It's a short book

I like to write books that I personally enjoy reading: short and to the point. When I was researching information about visiting London with my kids, I didn't find what I was looking for. Most books were either too long or too detailed. All I cared about was whether something would be worth my entire family's time and whether we could fit that into our short trip. Because I didn't find a book that met my needs, I wrote this one.

2) It's thoroughly researched and planned

My day job is a project management office director at Cisco Systems (lawyer-required note: views expressed in this guide are my own). In other words, I plan *everything.* When I was preparing for my trip, I read hundreds of online reviews and blog posts about things to do. I also read a few books about traveling in London with children, and I asked friends and colleagues what they personally enjoyed while on their trips. I then cross-checked all those recommendations to balance the must-see highlights with the family-friendly destinations. The end product of all that analysis is in this book.

3) It helps with avoiding FOMO and FOBO

FOMO stands for "Fear of Missing Out" and FOBO stands for "Fear of Better Options." FOMO and FOBO are your enemies during travel because they add unwanted stress. With only a few days, you will undoubtedly feel like you're going to miss out on something that wasn't part of your plan. This book will help you minimize both FOMO and FOBO because the research has been done on your behalf.

Some caveats

Here are a few things I'd like to point out before you continue reading:

- **This is NOT an extensive travel guide**. This book is not meant to cover everything you can possibly do in London. It is designed to solve a specific problem for parents who have limited time to plan for their trip. This means that a few activities and landmarks have been intentionally left out. For example, the Tower of London is not listed anywhere in the itinerary because most of the reviews I read stated that it's not the most family-friendly destination due to long wait lines and very little entertainment value for kids.

- **You can do everything in two full days**. This step-by-step guide is designed for a full weekend, starting on a Friday afternoon and continuing through Sunday evening (i.e., two and a half days). However, I have intentionally included an extra half day as a backup, making the plan flexible enough that it can be completed in just two days if necessary (e.g., Saturday morning through Sunday evening).

- **The activities are gender-neutral**. I have two little girls, and I planned my trip with them in mind. However, the activities are gender-neutral and work for both boys and girls. The activities also work if you have more than two kids.

- **The itinerary is summer-specific**. We visited London in late June, so the itinerary focuses on summer activities. Although most of the same landmarks and restaurants could be visited during winter as well, keep in mind that things like public parks might be less exciting during the colder months.

With that, let's get started with your trip!

Your Free Bonus

As a thank you for purchasing this book, I have included a free gift for you.

I have put together a small PDF file that shows you several cool maps of everything I cover in this book.

The maps highlight the different zones, landmarks, and walking paths in London that I discuss in my step-by-step plan.

You don't *need* to download this complimentary PDF file, as all the information you need is listed in the text.

However, it is a great supplement that lets you visually see the different places I refer to, especially since it's presented in the same day-by-day format listed in this book.

Visit the following page to download your free bonus:

www.thecouchmanager.com/liwbonus

Three Things to Do Before Your Trip

Here are three things that I recommend you do before your trip:

1) Download these free phone applications (iPhone or Android)

Google Maps – This was my go-to phone application that I used most of the time in London. Google Maps is the best GPS navigation app that gives you addresses for all your landmarks and shows you the shortest path for getting from one place to another. It also gives you driving, walking, and public transportation options, depending on your preference.

TripAdvisor – This application gives you user-generated reviews and pictures of restaurants and things to do in London. It uses your location to send you personalized recommendations of nearby places based on input by other travelers. I also used it whenever I wanted to read about famous historic sites that were around us.

Make sure you download these apps ahead

of time and familiarize yourself with their features *before* you get to London. The last thing you want to do is waste valuable time figuring out how to use them *while* you're in London.

Also, note that these apps require access to the Internet to work, so sign up for an international data plan before you go, or purchase a local mobile phone data plan when you arrive.

2) Buy the following essentials

I won't get into a laundry list of things to buy for your trip, but here are a few items that were extremely helpful for us when we got there:

Travel ID bracelets – It takes a split second for you to lose sight of your kids in touristy places. Buy a few disposable travel ID bracelets that the children can wear around their wrists or ankles in case they go missing. You can write down the name of your hotel, phone number, and any other information for law enforcement to contact you.

Hats & comfortable shoes – You'll be doing a lot of walking in London. Dress appropriately by wearing breathable hats and comfortable walking shoes, especially in mid-summer, when the weather gets quite warm.

Rain ponchos or light jackets – London has unpredictable weather. One minute, the sun is up and shining, and the next, the temperature drops and it starts pouring. It's a good idea to carry light jackets or rain ponchos so that you're prepared.

Portable battery pack – If you're going to use your smartphone for navigation and for photos, you'll probably drain your battery throughout the day. A portable battery pack will let you charge your phone (and other devices) on the go and avoid wasting time waiting for it to recharge.

International chargers/travel adapters (110V vs. 220V) – If you live in the U.S., then your electronic jacks will not fit into the European ones, so you'll need an adapter to be compatible. You'll also need a transformer if your device isn't dual-voltage ready (accepts 110V and 220V).

Backpack & small number lock – Everyone warns of London's pickpockets who can snatch your wallet or phone in an instant. We carried a backpack and kept all our money and valuables tucked safely inside with a number lock on the zipper.

Although unlocking and locking the backpack made it a bit of a hassle every time we needed to pay for something, it was much better than having to check our pockets every two minutes to make sure we hadn't been robbed. Get a backpack that has pouches on the sides to carry your kids' water bottles.

Travel credit card & British pounds – To avoid foreign transaction fees, sign up for a credit card that waives them for you. A couple that I've used are the Bank of America® Travel Rewards credit card and Chase Sapphire Preferred® credit card. Another good idea is to purchase British pounds before your trip (your local bank can provide this service). Although it's usually cheaper to purchase British currency after you land in London, having a couple of hundred pounds in your pocket before you arrive is a good idea—especially for the cab from the airport.

3) Get your kids excited about the trip

The final thing you should do before your trip is to get your kids excited about it early on so that they're passionately looking forward to it.

You can do that by sharing with them what you're going to do and see ahead of time.

For example, show them images of Hamleys or Big Ben using Google's image search. Or use Wikipedia to share interesting tidbits about the landmarks you'll see.

For young readers, you can even purchase an age-appropriate travel book that they can read themselves. *Kids' Travel Guide – London* was one that my ten-year-old particularly enjoyed.

Any investment in time to get them excited early on will definitely pay off later during your visit.

How I Planned the Weekend

Here's the strategy I followed to plan the weekend. You can skip this chapter if you want to, but I wanted to share my approach so that you get an idea of how to go about planning your own weekend if you'd like to make any changes.

First, I read a few books—and hundreds of reviews and blog posts—about places in London that were kid-friendly.

I then separated the "must-see" landmarks from the "nice-to-see" ones based on personal preference and how family-friendly they were. I also researched fun things to do (like tours or activities) and places to eat.

My approach to separating these two lists was simple. I wanted to do things that were authentic to the UK and London. When I came across things like Buckingham Palace (home of the Queen) or the London Eye (one of the world's tallest Ferris wheels), those went on the "must-see" list because there was no way we could experience them anywhere else.

However, when I came across things like the

Sea Life Aquarium (an aquarium in London) or Burger & Lobster (a restaurant known for its tasty lobster rolls), those went on the "nice-to-see" list because we had visited several aquariums, and we could eat awesome lobster rolls back in the U.S. These attractions would serve as back-up destinations in case our primary plan failed, or we needed to take a detour.

After that, I started plotting "must-see" landmarks and activities on a map and grouping them in zones to make our itinerary as efficient as possible. I also included places to eat along those paths.

Based on all of that, I ended up with four zones:

- **Zone 1**: Oxford Street, Hamleys, Leicester Square, and Covent Garden
- **Zone 2**: Buckingham Palace, Big Ben, London Eye, and the Thames River
- **Zone 3**: ZSL London Zoo and Camden Market
- **Zone 4**: Hyde Park, Harrods, and St. Ermin's Tea Lounge

Each zone includes "must-see" landmarks and activities that are within walking distance of each other (or a quick train ride) and can be visited within half a day.

On Friday afternoon, we did Zone 1. On Saturday, we did Zone 2 in the morning and Zone 3 in the afternoon. Then, on Sunday morning, we did Zone 4.

We left Sunday afternoon as a backup for unforeseen events, like getting hit with bad weather one day or waking up late on another.

In between zones, we sometimes took a break from the walking to go back to our hotel and relax. We stayed at the London Marriott Hotel Marble Arch (address: *134 George St, Marylebone, London W1H 5DN, UK*), which is close to Zones 1 and 4.

For transportation, we went in and out of the zones by the London Underground public transportation network (referred to by locals as "The Tube") because that was the most practical for us as a family. The London Underground system is very convenient, and we were never more than a five-minute walk away from a station when we needed one. You can purchase tickets at any station, and your best bet is to purchase an Oyster card, a reloadable card that gives you access to both the Tube and the double-decker buses (which are a lot of fun for kids). The Oyster card also has a cap on it, which means you don't have to pay any more after a certain daily limit is reached. Plus, children under 11 travel for free with a paying adult.

Read up on the transit system ahead of time on the "Transport for London" website (the integrated transport authority of London) at *https://tfl.gov.uk/* so that you understand how everything works.

In the next five chapters, I cover exactly what we did during each half-day.

Friday Afternoon

Spend your Friday afternoon in Zone 1, which includes Oxford Street, Hamleys, Leicester Square, and Covent Garden. You'll get a great first impression of the city and taste some amazing fish and chips. We left the hotel at around 2:30 p.m. and returned around 8:30 p.m., so we spent around six hours in this zone.

Oxford Street

What is it? Popular street
Address: *548 Oxford St, London W1C 1LU, UK*
Hours: Mon–Sun, 24 hours a day
Admission: Free
Recommended Duration: About 20 minutes

Kick-off your visit to London on Oxford Street, a famous street that is full of retail shops. Oxford Street is the busiest street in all of Europe and is considered a shopper's paradise. It is littered with luxury shops such as Louis Vuitton and Swarovski, as well as department stores such as John Lewis and Marks & Spencer. There are also a few souvenir shops sprinkled along the way.

Start your walk on Oxford Street from Marble Arch, a beautiful triumphal arch that was originally designed to be an entrance to Buckingham Palace. Then walk east as you spend some time doing some window shopping.

The street can get crowded because it's a tourist magnet, but it was fun for the kids to absorb the vibe of the city. They also loved watching the constant flow of red double-decker buses shuttling Londoners around.

The Mayfair Chippy

What is it? Popular fish and chips restaurant
Address: *14 North Audley Street, Mayfair, London W1K 6WE, UK*
Hours: Mon–Fri, 11:30 a.m.–9:45 p.m. | Sat–Sun, 11:00 a.m.–9:45 p.m.
Price: Around £14.00 for a Mayfair Classic Fish & Chips meal
Recommended Duration: About 1 hour

As you continue on Oxford street, keep walking until you hit N Audley Street and then make a right. The Mayfair Chippy will be a couple of blocks on your left.

A visit to London would not be complete without having a traditional fish and chips meal. Prior to our trip, I spent countless hours researching the best place to eat the classic British staple, and The Mayfair Chippy constantly ranked at the top according to several blogs and review sites.

I highly recommend you make a reservation before you go because the wait times can be quite long.

The restaurant serves two types of fish—cod and haddock—that are deep-fried in beer batter. My wife and I ordered both types of fish to share, and they were equally delicious, so you can't go wrong with either one. However, the haddock seems to be the more common local pick, so you might want to choose that if you're undecided.

Make sure you order their "Mayfair Classic," which includes your fried fish and chips, as well as a selection of three fantastic dipping sauces: mushy peas, tartar sauce, and curry sauce, all served on a beautiful platter.

After you're done, head back north on N Audley Street and turn right on Oxford Street. Continue walking east until you get to Ben's Cookies on your right (address: *Units 1-2, Sedley Pl, London W1C 2AE, UK*). This is a popular dessert shop that serves some of the freshest and most incredible cookies we've ever had. Try their milk chocolate chunk and triple chocolate chunk flavors (their melt-in-your-mouth cookies are big enough to share with your kids).

Across the street from Ben's Cookies is the Disney store (address: *350-352 Oxford St, London W1C 1JH, UK*) if you'd like to make a quick stop there.

Hamleys

What is it? Famous toy store
Address: *188-196 Regent St, Soho, London W1B 5BT, UK*
Hours: Mon–Fri, 10:00 a.m.–9:00 p.m. | Sat, 9:30 a.m.–9:00 p.m. | Sun, 12:00 p.m.–6:00 p.m.
Admission: Free to enter (toy prices vary)
Recommended Duration: About 45 minutes

After Ben's Cookies, continue to walk east on Oxford Street, and then make a right on Regent Street. Hamleys will be a few blocks on your left.

Hamleys is one of the oldest toy companies,

and their famous flagship store on Regent Street is the largest in the world, covering over 54,000 square feet (5,000 square meters) and spanning seven floors. Each floor has a different theme, and you'll find a toy that satisfies every child. There were sections for Star Wars, Harry Potter, Game of Thrones, Build-a-Bear, Barbie, and much, much more.

The things the kids enjoyed the most were the staff demonstrations. Employees were spread all around the store giving fun demonstrations about the toys, including magic tricks and flying drones. It was like free entertainment.

Leicester Square (via Piccadilly Circus)

What is it? Pedestrian square
Address: *Leicester Square, London WC2H 7LU, UK*
Hours: Mon–Sun, 24 hours a day
Price: Free
Recommended Duration: About 1.5 hours

After Hamleys, continue south on Regent Street and follow the path as it curves left until you reach Piccadilly Circus.

Piccadilly Circus is a major traffic junction of five intersecting streets. It is famous for its neon signs and bright displays, and, because of its busy tourist ambiance, some refer to it as the "Times Square of London," albeit a bit smaller.

Spend a few minutes taking pictures, particularly of the famous Shaftesbury Memorial Fountain that is topped with a winged bronze statue of *Anteros* (which is mistakenly referred to as the statue of *Eros* locally).

After Piccadilly Circus, head east on Coventry Street for a few blocks until you reach Leicester Square.

Leicester Square (pronounced "Less-ter"), is a vibrant pedestrian square that is surrounded by shops, restaurants, and theaters.

As you enter the square, there's a famous Lego toy shop on your right and an M&M's World chocolate shop on your left. Both stores are several stories high, and the kids had a blast visiting them. There's also a TWG tea store right next to the Lego store if you'd like to explore some of London's famous tea varieties.

Right in the middle of the square is where

street performers and musicians gather for some fun shows. The square can get overcrowded, but it is a must-see that allows the whole family to sit and enjoy the London vibes.

Covent Garden

What is it? Shopping and tourist site
Address: *The Market, Covent Garden, London WC2E 8RA, UK*
Hours: Mon–Sat, 10:00 a.m.–8:00 p.m. | Sun, 11:00 a.m.–6:00 p.m.
Admission: Free
Recommended Duration: About 2 hours

After Leicester Square, walk east on Cranbourn Street for a couple of blocks, which turns slightly right and becomes Garrick Street. Continue on Garrick Street, and then make a left on King Street until you reach the open space entrance to Covent Garden on your right.

Covent Garden is a popular shopping and entertainment site that is a joy to stroll around in. This is a perfect spot to people-watch and take some Instagram-able pictures of beautiful flower displays.

Start with the covered part of the market to check out stalls of crafts and cafes. There are also a lot of street performers and musicians (including opera singers) to keep the kids entertained.

Then cross over to the Jubilee Market that includes everything from handmade jewelry to food products.

When you're hungry, head over to Byron's Burgers (address: *33-35, Wellington St, Covent Garden, London WC2E 7BN, UK*) to have one of London's popular British beef burgers. Finish off your meal with their incredible "Oreo Freakshake," a milkshake topped with ice cream, a piece of cheesecake, and Oreo cookies. Your kids will love it.

Then head over to Trafalgar Square (address: *Trafalgar Square, Charing Cross, London WC2N 5DN, UK*) as your last stop for the day. Trafalgar Square is a public square that commemorates the Battle of Trafalgar during the historic Napoleonic Wars. Nelson's Column stands in the front of the square, surrounded by fountains and statues of mermaids, dolphins, and tritons. Relax on the steps as you enjoy the atmosphere and the sights of people walking around before heading back to your hotel and calling it a day.

Saturday Morning

Spend your Saturday morning in Zone 2, which includes Buckingham Palace, Big Ben, London Eye, and the Thames River. We left the hotel at around 9:30 a.m. and ended at around 2:00 p.m., so we spent about five hours in this zone. Keep in mind that this day is on a tight schedule because there are events that occur at specific times (like the Changing the Guard ceremony) or events that need ticket reservations (like the Thames River cruise), so you will need to plan ahead carefully.

St. James's Park

What is it? Royal park
Address: *St. James's Park, London SW1A 2BJ, UK*
Hours: Mon–Sun, 5:00 a.m.–12:00 a.m.
Admission: Free
Recommended Duration: About 30 minutes

Start your day at St. James's Park, a gorgeous 57-acre park that is located directly in front of Buckingham Palace.

The park is famous for its wildlife, including ducks, geese, swans, and pelicans. The viewing bridge over the lake in the middle of the park gives you a view of the London Eye in the distance and is a great spot to birdwatch and take pictures.

Make sure you're extra cautious about pickpockets in this particular area. I recall the police walking by every few minutes and pleading that we continuously watch our bags.

Then head over to a small playground in the southwest corner for the kids to enjoy before hopping over to see the famous flower beds (also known as the Memorial Gardens) that are laid out in front of Buckingham Palace.

Buckingham Palace (Changing the Guard Ceremony)

What is it? The Queen's home and guard ceremony
Address: *Buckingham Palace, London SW1A 1AA, UK*
Hours: Mon–Sun, 11:00 a.m. (please check the official times first because schedules can change on short notice)
Price: Free

Recommended Duration: About 45 minutes

As you stand next to the flower beds in St. James's Park, you can view Buckingham Palace with all the glory of the Victoria Memorial (a monument to Queen Victoria) in front of you.

Buckingham Palace houses the residence and administrative offices of the royal family. It's basically the home of the Queen, and the place where people gather for major celebrations.

You can tour Buckingham Palace by purchasing tickets ahead of time, but we decided to skip that because we thought it wouldn't be very exciting for the kids.

What we didn't want to miss, though, was the famous "Changing the Guard" ceremony that starts at 11:00 a.m. local time every day of the week (check official times on their website, as schedules might change: *https://www.householddivision.org.uk/inde x.php?action=changing-the-guard-calendar*).

The Queen's Guard are the soldiers who are responsible for protecting the official royal residences in the UK. They're infantry that wear the famous uniforms of red jackets and black bearskin hats.

The Changing the Guard ceremony highlights how The Old Guard hands over responsibility to the New Guard.

There are two ways for you to watch the ceremony. The first is to stand right in front of the palace, where you can watch the New Guard relieving the Old Guard. According to many reviews, this is the best place to view the event. However, if you want to get a good view, you have to arrive very early to secure a spot. It gets really crowded, and the guards are too far away to see very clearly.

The second way is more kid-friendly (you don't have to get there super early), and it also lets you avoid the huge crowds. Timing, however, is everything, so here's what you need to do.

At around 10:20 a.m., head south to the Wellington Barracks, which are at the end of Birdcage Walk Street. There, you'll see the New Guard being inspected as the regimental band plays some music. You can spend around 25 minutes listening to the band and watching guards conduct marches across the yard.

Then, at exactly 10:57 a.m., the soldiers will march out of the barracks gates and turn left to head over to Buckingham Palace. A great spot to stand with your kids is just to the side of the gates before they open. We took up position at exactly 10:50 a.m. and were able to see them just a few feet away as they marched out. To see the exact location I'm referring to, make sure you download the map that I referenced earlier (available at: *www.thecouchmanager.com/liwbonus*).

You can follow the guards to the palace as they march out of the gate, but it'll get crowded, and you won't be able to see anything anyway. Instead, you can quickly head back north through St. James's Park, then make a left at The Mall Road, and wait at the corner of The Mall Road and Stable Yard Road. At exactly 11:10 a.m., you'll see another small group of guards marching east and turning left on Stable Yard Road to relieve sentries who have been standing guard at St James's Palace, which was a nice bonus.

After researching reviews and blog posts, we opted for this second way. And we were not disappointed at all. My kids had a blast, and we were able to get quite close to the soldiers. The best part was that the kids were able to listen to the live band, which was a lot of fun.

There are other events and ceremonies that take place, like the Household Cavalry at around 11:35 a.m. or another band march at around 11:45 a.m., but we decided we were satisfied with what we had seen and headed on to our next landmark.

Big Ben

What is it? Bell of the clock inside Elizabeth Tower
Address: *Westminster, London SW1A 0AA, UK*
Hours: Mon–Sun, 24 hours a day
Price: Free
Recommended Duration: About 20 minutes

After the ceremony, head east on The Mall Road and make a right again back into St. James's Park. If you're due for a treat, there's a little café on your right that sells famous soft-serve vanilla ice cream cones with Flake chocolate bars (made by Cadbury, the British confectionery company) sticking out of the sides. These cones are pretty popular around parks in London, and you should have at least one during your trip.

Then head east through the park, turning south around the lake and make a quick stop at Duck Island Cottage, a small historic cottage with pretty gardens.

Afterward, continue south within the park, and make a left on Birdcage Walk Street. Keep walking east on Birdcage Walk Street for a block or so, which turns into Great George Street, and then make a right on Parliament Square.

Parliament Square is a square where Londoners usually hold protests, and it features statues of notable individuals, including Abraham Lincoln, Winston Churchill, and Mahatma Gandhi. On the south end of the square is Westminster Abbey, a large church and burial site for monarchs.

We didn't enter Westminster Abbey because we knew it wouldn't be very thrilling for the kids, but we did take some nice pictures of the Gothic architecture.

After Parliament Square, head east on Great George Street, which becomes Bridge Street, and you'll see Big Ben on your right.

Big Ben is the name given to the huge bell of the clock inside Elizabeth Tower, which sits at the north end of the Houses of Parliament. It's the iconic clock tower that you see on nearly every London postcard, and you shouldn't miss it.

Unfortunately for us, Big Ben was under a four-year restoration project when we visited, and we were disappointed because we could barely see anything except for one of the clock faces peeking out from behind the scaffolding.

However, it should reopen in 2021. If you visit after it does, make sure you wait around to listen to the chimes that go off every 15 minutes. At the top of every hour, you can also hear the actual Big Ben bell signaling the hour of the day.

London Eye + Thames River Cruise

What is it? Observation wheel and river cruise
Address: *Riverside Building, Westminster Bridge Rd., London SE1 7PB*
Hours: Mon–Sun, 10:00 a.m.–8:30 p.m. (opening times could vary depending on the day and month, see *https://www.londoneye.com/* for more details)
Price: Around £120.00 for combo tickets (London Eye + cruise) for a family of four
Recommended Duration: About 2 to 3 hours

After Big Ben, continue onto Westminster Bridge Road, and then make a left at the end of the bridge at The Queen's Walk to get to the Coca-Cola London Eye.

The London Eye is one of the largest observation wheels in the world. It's 443 feet (135 meters) high and includes 32 passenger capsules that rotate at a steady pace. It takes around 30 minutes for the wheel to make a full revolution (you only go around once).

The kids loved the ride because they could walk around freely in the sealed capsule while enjoying gorgeous 360-degree views of London.

It's also one of the most popular tourist attractions in the UK, and waiting lines can get insanely long, so it's best if you plan ahead by purchasing tickets before you get there (you'll still wait with tickets, but it will be a much shorter wait). Doing so will also help you manage your schedule better so you don't end up losing the entire afternoon sitting around waiting with restless kids.

The easiest way to buy tickets is through the London Eye's main website at *https://www.londoneye.com/*. They have special combination ticket deals, and I recommend that you purchase a combined

London Eye and river cruise deal. You'll receive a special family discount and get to enjoy London from the sky *and* the water.

Keep in mind that both tickets (for the London Eye and the river cruise) are timed, which means that you'll need to factor in waiting times and delays between both attractions when you book them. My advice is to keep a buffer of around 1.5 to 2 hours between the start times of each attraction. For example, if your listed "arrival time" (printed on your ticket) at the London Eye is between 11:45 a.m. and 12:00 p.m., then you should book the Thames River Cruise sometime between 1:15 p.m. and 1:45 p.m.

That's because you should expect to wait around 30 to 45 minutes in line to get on the London Eye after your arrival time, and you don't want to miss your river cruise.

The good news is that the cruise departure point is right next to the London Eye, so you don't have to waste time commuting there. And if you are done early and end up with some free time between attractions, then you can spend that extra time watching a free 4D movie about the London Eye (included with your ticket) in the nearby theater next to the sales office.

The cruise takes around 40 minutes, and it

passes by some of the most important landmarks along the River Thames, including Shakespeare's Globe, the HMS Belfast, and the Tower of London. The most exciting landmarks for the kids were the London Bridge (from the famous lullaby) as well as the Tower Bridge (the iconic bascule and suspension bridge).

The cruise was great because it saved us from taking separate trips to all those locations, and the live commentary by the guides helped explain some fun facts about all those landmarks.

After the cruise, head over to Fishcotheque for lunch (address: *79A Waterloo Rd, Lambeth, London SE1 8UD, UK*). Fishcotheque was the second-highest rated fish and chips restaurant according to my research (after The Mayfair Chippy).

Note: After lunch, you can head over to your hotel to rest for a little bit. On every trip, I usually find it refreshing to return to the hotel in the middle of the day so that the kids can rest their tired feet or take a short nap. However, on this particular day, we had to skip taking a break because of the timed tickets in the morning and the early closing times of our afternoon activities.

Saturday Afternoon

Spend your Saturday afternoon and evening in Zone 3, which includes the area around London Zoo and Camden Market. We started at around 2:30 p.m. and returned later in the evening at around 8:00 p.m., so we spent approximately five and a half hours in Zone 3.

ZSL London Zoo

What is it? London's main zoo
Address: *Outer Cir, London NW1 4RY, UK*
Hours: Mon–Sun, 10:00 a.m.–varies (check *https://www.zsl.org/* for seasonal closing times)
Admission: Around £27.00 per adult/ £18.00 for children 3 to 15 years old
Recommended Duration: About 2 hours

ZSL London Zoo one of the world's oldest scientific zoos. Although I don't usually get excited about zoo trips when we're on a short trip (because they typically eat up an entire half-day that could be spent elsewhere), London's main zoo was perfect because of its fairly small size and proximity to Camden Market.

It's a highly rated zoo that only took us around two hours to complete.

Here were some of the kids' favorite exhibits:

- **Reptile House**: A great collection of snakes, lizards, and frogs. You'll find the location of the scene from the first Harry Potter movie, where the python speaks to Harry and escapes from its glass enclosure.
- **Penguin Beach**: An exhibit that recreates a South American beach, and includes under- and over-water viewing areas to watch how the penguins swim and interact.
- **Butterfly Paradise**: A variety of free-flying butterflies and moths from all around the world. The enclosure is heated to provide the right temperature for the insects.
- **B.U.G.S.**: A biodiversity and educational exhibit (B.U.G.S. stands for Biodiversity Underpinning Global Survival) that showcases several insects and arachnids. My daughters enjoyed watching the locusts and the spiders. The spiders, surprisingly, were roaming freely in one giant enclosure, so if you have a fear of them, you might want to stay away

from this exhibit!

- **Land of the Lions**: A highly-reviewed exhibit that has a theme based on India's Gir National Park. The layout is well-designed, and you can view the lions up close in great detail.

Make sure you also check out the zoo's daily activities schedule on their website (at *https://www.zsl.org/zsl-london-zoo/visitor-information/zoo-activities*) because they have several demonstrations and live feedings planned. We enjoyed watching an "Animals in Action" show featuring a few climbing and flying animals in the outdoor amphitheater.

Camden Market

What is it? Collection of food stalls, cafes, and shops
Address: *Camden Lock Place, London NW1 8AF, UK*
Hours: Mon–Sun, 10:00 a.m.–6:00 p.m.
Price: Prices vary
Recommended Duration: About 2 hours

After the London Zoo, head east on Outer Circle and then make a left on The Broad Walk. After you cross a small bridge, make a right on Prince Albert Road and then another right to take the footpath. At the end of the ramp, make a left to head north along the bank of Regent's Canal.

This short 15-minute walk was a nice, unplanned surprise for us because we didn't expect to see a colorful collection of narrow canal boats lined up along the sides. These charming boats, no wider than around four feet, looked like they served as tiny houses and small businesses (barbers and bookshops) for some of the locals, and they were magnificent to look at.

As you continue north on the canal, you'll cross another small bridge, and then make a left on Camden High Street until you get to Camden Market on your left.

Camden Market is a huge market full of unique food stalls, shops, and cafés. It's an eclectic, trendy place with a lot of artwork and dinner options to check out and choose from. This was one of our favorite spots in London.

Start by strolling around and enjoying the hustle and bustle of the different stalls and vendors. Make sure you check out Gin Alley, where many local artists display their work. There's also a famous statue of Amy Winehouse close by.

When you're hungry, you'll find an

overwhelming selection of street food options to choose from, but here are a few suggestions.

For dinner, try either The Mac Factory (*http://www.themacfactory.co.uk/*), which specializes in mac n cheese dishes, or VBurger (*https://vburger.co.uk/*), which sells delicious plant-based burgers.

For dessert, the kids might love a nostalgic cereal bowl from the Cereal Killer Café (*https://www.cerealkillercafe.co.uk/*), or an ice cream made with liquid nitrogen from Chin Chin (*https://chinchinicecream.com/*).

The Harry Potter Shop at Platform 9¾

What is it? A Harry Potter merchandise store
Address: *Kings Cross Station, Kings Cross, London N1 9AP, UK*
Hours: Mon–Sat, 8:00 a.m.–10:00 p.m. | Sun, 9:00 a.m.–9:00 p.m.
Admission: Free to visit
Recommended Duration: About 45 minutes

As you wrap up your evening and head back to the hotel, make a quick stop at

King's Cross station to visit The Harry Potter Shop at Platform 9¾.

King's Cross station is a bit of a hike from Camden Market (it takes around 35 minutes), so it's best if you take the Tube from Camden Town station.

The Harry Potter Shop is a great attraction for all Harry Potter fans. It's a store that sells Harry Potter merchandise and collectibles, including some products that are exclusive to the store. You'll find souvenirs, clothes, and plush toys from the Wizarding World of Harry Potter.

The most notable thing about the shop is its location right next to the actual train platforms nine and ten. There's also a great photo opportunity with a luggage trolley half-buried into a wall, allowing you to mimic the scenes where Harry and others run through the wall to board the Hogwarts Express.

You can pose for a picture next to the trolley while wearing a scarf and holding a wand that are provided by the staff. However, the lines can get quite long, so you might want to factor in around a 30-minute wait if your kids are interested.

After the shop, head back to the hotel to

call it a day.

Sunday Morning

Spend your Sunday morning in Zone 4, which includes Hyde Park and Harrods. We left the hotel at around 8:30 a.m. and returned at around 1:30 p.m., so we spent five hours in this zone.

Hyde Park

What is it? Largest royal park
Address: *Marble Arch, London W1H 7EJ, UK*
Hours: Mon–Sun, 5:00 a.m.–12:00 a.m.
Price: Free
Recommended Duration: About 2 to 3 hours

Hyde Park is a gorgeous park that feels like an oasis in the middle of the city. It is London's largest royal park, and it's so huge that you can spend an entire day without fully covering it all.

Start your morning by having a quick breakfast at the nearby GAIL's bakery (address: *4-6 Seymour Pl, Marylebone, London W1H 7NA, UK*), a popular bakery chain in London. They serve warm, freshly baked bread every day, and you can't go wrong with any of their mouth-watering pastries (see *https://gailsbread.co.uk/* for more details).

Then head over to Hyde Park's northeast entrance through Marble Arch to check out Speakers' Corner. This section of the park is the birthplace of public speaking and open debate. Every Sunday morning, crowds gather to listen to speakers talk about their different views, and it's a great experience to teach your kids about the origins of free speech and lawful protest.

After Speakers' Corner, head over to the Serpentine, a stunning lake where you can rent a four-person paddle boat and absorb the picturesque scenery from the water (the boathouse on the Serpentine opens at 10:00 a.m.). Kids will have a great time watching the swans, ducks, and other birds swimming around. The fee is around £12.00 per adult and £5.00 per child for a one-hour ride.

Surprisingly, there were no restrictions on feeding the birds (this is usually forbidden in the United States, where you're asked not to feed any animals in public parks), so you might want to come prepared with a few bird-friendly snacks. The birds were so used to people feeding them that they ate out of my daughters' hands while we were paddling on the water.

After the paddle boat ride, check out the nearby Princess Diana Memorial Fountain, a cascading water flow dedicated to the late Princess of Wales. Close to the memorial is an outdoor playground with climbing frames that is fun for the kids to spend some time in.

Harrods

What is it? World-famous department store
Address: *87-135 Brompton Road Knightsbridge London SW1X 7XL, UK*
Hours: Mon–Sat, 10:00 a.m.–9:00 p.m. | Sun, 11:30 a.m.–6:00 p.m.
Admission: Free
Recommended Duration: About 1 hour

After Hyde Park, head south toward S Carriage Drive and cross the street to continue to Park Close. Stay heading south (Park Close becomes Knightsbridge Green), and then make a right on Brompton Road. Harrods is located a block or so on your left.

Harrods is a luxury department store famous for its high-end retail shops. If you're looking to shop for luxury brand items, you'll find plenty here. The reviews I researched all seemed to agree that prices are set to match the fancy atmosphere, so we didn't plan on actually purchasing anything. However, because it's such a popular tourist destination and also within easy striking distance of Hyde Park, we decided to stop by and enjoy some quality window shopping.

The store is huge, and you can easily get lost trying to find your way around, so make sure you grab one of their free maps.

A few things that we thought were worth seeing included the Egyptian Escalator, which is a series of beautifully crafted escalators that showcase statues and reliefs of ancient Egypt. Make sure you check out Princess Diana and Dodi Fayed's memorial at the base of the escalator.

Another popular destination at Harrod's is their top-notch food hall. This is a high-end food court unlike any we've ever seen. It's very well presented, and the food displays look super scrumptious. Everything looked outstanding, and it was a feast for the eyes.

Finally, the girls also enjoyed visiting the children's toy floor, where there were a lot of demonstrations going on (similar to Hamleys) that kept them entertained. On that same floor is the Harrods Tea Rooms, which is worth checking out as well.

St. Ermin's Tea Lounge

What is it? Afternoon tea lounge
Address: *Caxton St, Westminster, London SW1H 0QW, UK*
Hours: Mon–Sun, 12:00 p.m.–5:00 p.m.
Price: Around £30.00 per adult/ £18.00 per child
Recommended Duration: About 1 hour

After Harrods, take the bus or the Tube to head toward St. Ermin's Hotel. You can walk there, but it'll take you around 30 minutes, so it's best if you take public transportation.

St. Ermin's Hotel is a hotel that's part of the luxurious Autograph Collection, and they have a fantastic afternoon tea lounge.

In Britain, afternoon tea refers to a small meal between lunch and dinner (not just the drink). The meal typically includes finger sandwiches, scones, clotted cream, and a selection of pastries—all served on an extravagant three-tiered plate stand. It's a local tradition that Londoners enjoy on special occasions, and we wanted to experience the fun ritual.

There are hundreds of options for afternoon tea locations around London, and, as I was researching for one, I focused my criteria on two things. First, I wanted a kid-friendly place. Second, I wanted a venue that didn't require a formal dress code. Some tea rooms were too restrictive about what we could wear, and I didn't want to waste time going back to the hotel to change into formal clothes. I was also looking for a place that was fancy enough for us to enjoy the true experience, but not too fancy where we'd feel uncomfortable with our kids.

St. Ermin's Tea Lounge met both those requirements. Not only did they have an amazing upscale setting, but they were so welcoming of kids that they even had tailored child menus.

Their service and food were impeccable, and I highly recommend it. You will need to make reservations ahead of time, and my suggestion is to book your experience directly through their website at *https://www.sterminshotel.co.uk/eating-drinking/afternoon-tea/*

After St. Ermin's, head back to the hotel to get some rest and freshen up.

Sunday Afternoon

Sunday afternoon was left as a backup to plan for events that were beyond our control. If our flight was delayed on Friday, or if it rained on Saturday, we would have used our Sunday afternoon to make up for any lost time.

We also wanted to allow for some flexibility in case we wanted to sleep in late one day or spend more time in a location because we were enjoying our time.

I highly recommend you do this as well because it'll help you enjoy your vacation and not stress out about anything you might miss. Having a backup scheduled by design becomes especially valuable if one of your kids gets sick or cranky, and you need to deviate from your plan to get them back on track.

Assuming everything goes smoothly for you, though, you'll have an entire half-day at your disposal.

You can spend it on any of the "nice-to-see" places from your earlier list or on a return trip to a zone you already visited. Some landmarks, such as Big Ben, have a different look and feel in the evening when the lights are on.

So what can you do?

Here are my recommendations.

First, visit the British Museum. This was already on our "nice-to-see" list, but we didn't have the time to squeeze it in earlier on. It's free to visit the museum (though donations are recommended).

My kids don't really enjoy museums, but the British Museum was special because it houses one of history's crown jewels, the Rosetta Stone.

The Rosetta Stone is the famous stone that helped decipher Egyptian hieroglyphics and consequently helped scholars unlock Egypt's ancient history. It's such a popular artifact that there's even a gift shop nearby dedicated to selling merchandise—including bags, pencils, and mugs—about the stone.

In addition to the Rosetta Stone, there are a few other highlights that are worth visiting. If you're short on time (and patience), the museum makes it easy for you by giving you a "one hour at the museum" plan. The plan covers all the must-see artifacts from around the world in under 60 minutes. You can grab a copy of the guide from the information desk.

After the museum, take the Tube to the Open Air Theatre at Regent's Park, where there are several plays scheduled in a stunning outdoor theater (check schedules at *https://openairtheatre.com/*). If that doesn't work out, you can visit the nearby Madame Tussauds London (address: *Marylebone Road, London NW1 5LR, UK*). This is a world-renowned wax museum that features lifelike wax statues of celebrities, including members of the Royal Family.

For dinner, grab some pizza from the nearby L'Antica Pizzeria da Michele (address: *48 Rue Madame, 75006 London, France*). This restaurant constantly showed up as one of the best pizza restaurants during my research. Try their double mozzarella, which seemed to be their most sought-after pizza.

Then head back to Regents Park to relax and wind down with the kids. Regents Park is the best place to wrap up your vacation as you absorb the last sights of people strolling around.

Conclusion

We just covered a step-by-step itinerary that will help you plan for your trip with your kids.

One suggestion I have is to go back to the beginning of the book and re-read the "Three Things to Do Before Your Trip" section. This will help you plan ahead and make sure you'll get the most out of your trip.

Then, as you get closer to your date of travel, I recommend that you check any potential closing dates of the main landmarks that you'll visit. Some of them, such as the London Eye, might be closed for planned renovations. Other landmarks might also be closed during public holidays. Knowing all this information ahead of time will help you modify your trip and avoid any potential disappointment.

Also, if you haven't done so already, make sure you download the complimentary PDF guide so you have a nice visual of the different paths you will take.

Visit the following page to download your

free bonus:

www.thecouchmanager.com/liwbonus

Finally, remember that FOMO (Fear of Missing Out) and FOBO (Fear of Better Options) are your enemies during your journey. The best trips are about who you're *with* and not about what you *do*. Even if things don't go 100% according to plan, don't lose focus on the big picture: you're in London and this is a vacation.

So enjoy it with your family.

Two Quick Requests!

I'd like to thank you once again for purchasing this book. I hope you found it helpful, and I wish you the best on your trip.

A couple of quick requests:

1) Please review the book on Amazon

If you enjoyed the book, please leave an honest review about it on Amazon. I know you probably get asked this a lot from most authors. However, every single review counts, and it would help me understand how to improve in my future books. Writing a review takes as little as sixty seconds, and, if you're unsure of what to write, let me know how one thing in this book has helped you. I read every single review and sincerely appreciate your feedback.

2) Check out my other books: "Rome in a Weekend with Two

Kids" and "Paris in a Weekend with Two Kids"

If you enjoyed reading this book, then you'll love my two other travel books:

Rome in a Weekend with Two Kids
Paris in a Weekend with Two Kids

They're written in the exact same style as this book and give you a great step-by-step itinerary of what you can do around the Italian and French capitals. I also highlight the absolute best places to eat, as well as where to go to enjoy some fun activities with your kids.

You can find the book on Amazon by searching for *Rome in a Weekend with Two Kids* or *Paris in a Weekend with Two Kids* in the search bar.

Thanks again!

Hassan

Would you like to write a book like this one?

This is my third travel book, and I wrote it while being a full-time employee, a full-time father, and a full-time procrastinator.

Writing a book is a process that's a lot easier than most people think.

In fact, I've written three other books as a part-time author.

If you would like to write a book like this one yourself, check out my latest Amazon #1 Best Seller:

Write Your Book on the Side: How to Write and Publish Your First Nonfiction Kindle Book While Working a Full-Time Job *(Even if You Don't Have a Lot of Time and Don't Know Where to Start)*

Here's what a few people have said about it:

"As a full-time Harvard Trauma surgeon, a full-time researcher and a full-time father of 3, I do not have the time to write a book on the side. Or so I thought. This book completely challenged my misconceptions

and deeply motivated me to write a book myself."
- Dr. Haytham Kaafarani, Assistant Professor of Surgery, Harvard Medical School

"Publishing your own book will help you clarify the message you want the world to hear. This concise, smart read shows you exactly how to do it, step-by-step."
- Dave Stachowiak, Host of the "Coaching for Leaders" podcast

"Highly readable, accessible, and positive, with practical tips and a systematic framework for the writing and publishing process."
- Rob Archangel, Owner and Co-founder of "Archangel Ink"

Visit the following link to check out my "Write Your Book on the Side" book:

www.thecouchmanager.com/bookontheside

Made in the USA
Las Vegas, NV
22 April 2024

89007601R00038